Theban Traffic

For Joyce,
Who knows how to
stay clear of
traffic —
Thank so much —
Walter Bargen

Other Books by Walter Bargen

West of West (2007)

Remedies for Vertigo (2006)

The Feast (2004)

Vow of Hunger (2003)

The Body of Water (2003)

Harmonic Balance (2001)

Water Breathing Air (1999)

At the Dead Center of Day (1997)

The Vertical River (1995)

Rising Waters: Year of the Great Flood (1993)

Yet Other Waters (1991)

Mysteries in the Public Domain (1990)

Fields of Thenar (1980)

Theban Traffic

Poems by Walter Bargen

Cherry Grove Collections

Walter Bargen
First Poet Laureate of Missouri
6/7/14

Published by Cherry Grove Collections
P.O. Box 541106
Cincinnati, OH 45254-1106

Typeset in Palatino by WordTech Communications LLC,
Cincinnati, OH

ISBN: 9781934999134
LCCN: 2008928601

Poetry Editor: Kevin Walzer
Business Editor: Lori Jareo

Visit us on the web at www.cherry-grove.com

The following poems, sometimes with different titles and in different forms, first appeared in the following journals and magazines:

Blue Mesa Review: "Betrayal"
Coal City Review: "Theban Cacophony"
In the Teeth of the Wind: "Stella Confesses to the
        Invention of Thebes"
Karamu: "Obnubliation"
Laurel Review: "Middle Way"
PIFMagazine.com: "Results & Prospects in
        Thebes"
MelicReview.com: "Theban Timing,"
        "Theban Ruins"
Mid-America Poetry Review: "How Tables Learn
        to Talk"
New Letters: "The Letter"
Puerto del Sol: "Asymmetry"
Quarter After Eight: "Nicked Names,"
        "Ungulated"
Rattle: "Theban Planet"
Red Rock Review: "Resume, "Hurdling Epic,"
        "Executing Fireflies"
Rio Grande Review: "Hearing Aid"
River King: "Cold Wet Morning"
Salt Hill Journal: "Theban Diaries"
Sentence: "Terrorist in Thebes"
Seattle Review: "Attila at Breakfast"

"Concerted Effort" appears in the Kearney Street Press anthology *Tribute to Orpheus,* 2007.

"Those Things" was awarded the 1996 Hanks Prize and appeared in the anthology *Fathers* published by St. Martin's Press.

Contents

A Brief Note 11
Riddled Prelude 15

Stella & Jake Awash in Thebes
Cold Wet Morning 19
New Waves on Old Water 20
Soggy News 21
Love Adrift 22
Marooned in Thebes 23
Flossing Shadows 24
Love Letter 25
Having to Ask 26
Fire Slapstick 27
A Very Cellular Birthday 28
Sailing Thebes 29
Vacuuming the Rich 30
Attila at Breakfast 31
Play It Again 32
Prestidigitation 33
No Help 34
Concerted Effort 36
Hearing Aid 37

Wildlife in Thebes
Ungulated 41
In the Trenches 42
Asymmetry 43
What Stella Doesn't Know About the Tailor 44
Betrayal 45

Endearments 47
Dated 48
Extasy 50
Obnubliation 52
Theban Ruins 54
Amputee 55
Blue Migration 57
How Tables Learn to Talk 59
Theban Timing 60
Theban Planet 62

Theban Traffic
Résumé 65
Sphinx 66
Hurdling Epic 67
Executing Fireflies 68
Those Things 69
Results & Prospects in Thebes 70
Theban Diaries 71
Hanging Gardens of Thebes 72
Theban Cacophony 73
Middle Way 74
Enlightenment Again 76
Sand Locust 77
Monastery 78
Trouble with the Egyptian Travel Agent 79
Terrorist in Thebes 84

Invention of Thebes
Nicked Name 87
Just Right 88
Thebedom Pigdom 90

Say Anything Theban 91
Waxing Ubermensch 92
Burning Bed 94
RSVP 95
Unemployed in Troy 96
Odyssey 97
Double-Yoked 98
Agog 99
Stella Confesses to the Invention of Thebes 100
Another Theban Day 104

A Brief Note

I never intended to write a book of poems that
required an introduction. How many times have I
heard poets ring the alarm :

A poem should not mean
but be.
>> Archibald MacLeish

and

Like a bowl of roses, a poem
should not have to be explained.
>> Lawrence Ferlinghetti

Sage advice that I wholly accept, but I should have
known that I was veering away from when my wife,
confronted with the title to this book, suggested that I
write a note to the reader, giving an explanation for
the use of ancient Greek mythology and place names
along with the conflation of multiple geographies,
including the United States, locations separated by
millennia.

Most of the poems take place within and around the
relationship between Stella & Jake, two people who
are wrapped in strife and love. Their relationship is

passionate but often out of step with each other. These conflicts are not unique to our era; they can be found in the tragedies and comedies of Sophocles, Euripides, Aeschylus, and Aristophanes. Of course, the external accouterments are different: BMW's have replaced chariots, KIA's have replaced donkey carts. Still, intellectually, artistically, politically, Western Civilization is the inheritor of much from ancient Greece.

Stella & Jake live in the city of Thebes. There are two small U.S. cities that have the same name, one in Arkansas, the other in Illinois. Stella & Jake's Thebes is neither one of these and both, along with the Thebes of Greece and Egypt. The conflation of place names is simply to remind us that what we feel, what we think, has deep tangled roots and hasn't changed much in all these centuries. It's also a reminder of the warning from E.M. Cioran: *All men who look after past ruins imagine for themselves that they can avoid the ruins to come.*

Different worlds, both equally offended.
Antigone by Sophocles

Everyone is raised by the gods
but we never learned our lines.
Jim Harrison

Riddled Prelude

Traffic stutters, stops, congested with the language of appointments, syntax of deals, the speeding present, glistening chrome futures, where right, left, and straight are clearly visible. He hoists himself onto the green bus bench. He struts back and forth above his idling congregation, facing down the exhaust-streaked walls of semi's. He looks up from the opened black book he balances chest high on his rigid left arm. His right arm swings down repeatedly splitting the grain of air, kindling the faith. The bounce of plastic-beaded necklaces cascades afternoon light over his black robes. In front of the Mexican Restaurant advertising a three-taco lunch special, he shouts to the holy wheeling street.

It's little different for the woman who cuddles and rocks her baby cradled in her left arm. When it's time for the child to crawl, to step away and grasp the world by the playful throat, the child uses only one small hand and arm. The other remains at its chubby side, as if the child is clairvoyant and already knows there is only one way to defy the riddle. Two greedy hands, an unnecessary complication and proselytizing takes only one good swing.

With two legs and one hand, the baby defies the sphinx. This time there is no Creon to claim a kingdom, no Jocasta equal to the weight of the answer, no Oedipus to haunt mothers for millennia. The diagnosis: stroke in the womb, a premature thunder clap that welded one arm in place, leaving only one hand to praise congested Theban traffic.

Stella & Jake Awash in Thebes

Cold Wet Morning

"It's called a Spartan shower," Jake shouts. That
doesn't stop the complaints pouring from the second
floor bathroom.

At first the slapping sounds innocent enough, school
of salmon leaping up the cataract of wooden stairs.
The house shakes, the medicine cabinet crashes to the
sink. Now there's a choice, three pink pills or three
shards of mirror to swallow.

The walls are thin enough to swim through. He hears
lunging: the shower curtain torn down, the gasping
gills of something trying to squeeze down the drain.

A fishy smell drifts along the hall into the kitchen.
Jake's lumpy oatmeal is pale as belly-up flounder
pounded on the rocks of Tristan de Cunha.

The door flung open, her hair slicked back, Stella
stands naked, an immaculate tuna blue, scales of ice
clinging to her eyebrows. In a salty soprano, she
sings, "We're drowning in two stories of cold."

New Waves on Old Water

Stella travels two thousand miles to sweep up the
dust of another relative. Whole mountain ranges pass
below her quicker than dreams. She perches on the
edge of a continent.

Because they cannot see each other, they cannot
exchange diseases though the distant unease is
worse. Though they cannot share a bottle of wine
their separate glasses overflow with a blush of light.
There is a smeared stain in the air like a burning city.
Over the phone, he hears her say that's the sun setting
over the Pacific.

The trees drop all their leaves. Each leaf falls into its
own winter. They heap up words so the fire will thaw
whatever has frozen. They throw children in and see
how brightly they burn: one in Mexico, one
repeatedly breaking his collar bone like a twig of
kindling. Another crosses borders, not to flee old
wars, but to escape into the skirmishes of marriage.

In a house facing west, Stella sits through the evening.
The relentless line of horizon breaks through her.
Waves claw the beach, dragging back the half-alive.
Slicking the sand, the tide arrives like a rash. Plumes
of water crown the tops of rocks. She feels a salty
spray blow across her face. Marooned in the forgotten
middle of a continent, Jake strolls uneasily looking
around at what they've forged of old seas.

Soggy News

He shakes the rain out of the Theban Times-Courier.
An inverted open umbrella in the corner is his life
boat. His crew abandoned him years ago. The entire
table to circumnavigate, his coffee cup steams toward
the edge.

He smooths out a sea-smear of cheap print. The
letters wriggle like grunions on a night beach: armed
robbery at the Seven Eleven drips onto his lap, a
trickle of family abuse, a persistent runnel of tax
evaders, a deep pool of obituaries. He stomps his peg
leg on the floor protesting the violent decline of
civilization. The macaw perched on his shoulder
squawks a call to arms and begs for a biscotti.

Love Adrift

In his plaid pajamas, Jake walks out of a tavern on the
cold slopes of Parnassus, where all the bottles are
filled with either three-masted ships or lighthouses.
He sways on the wet deck of the schooner he
swallowed. Tongue slick, his words are washed
overboard.

His skin's green as a stagnant pond. He slaps along
the sidewalk with a loose-webbed sole. Groggy, Jake's
searching for a bullfrog to kiss. He throws a weighted
rope into the current that runs under Main Street and
croaks Mark Twain to no one in particular. Before he
knows it, he's head-over-heels as Stella sails past
offering him a ride in her red '64 Mustang.

Marooned in Thebes

It wasn't until he coughed up a mouthful of salt
water, including a wriggling shrimp and a frilly
lionfish that had stuck under his tongue, that he knew
he'd washed up on the sea of her belly. He didn't
bother flossing the kelp, picking broken shells from
between his teeth, brushing sand from his sun-scaled
lips. Her soft flesh rose so slowly with her breathing,
and he sank so irrevocably, he didn't realize he was
submerged until he gasped for air as the sea rushed
up his nose. He was sucked deep into her navel
vortex. He choked as the descending curve of her
belly slid into dark space and the hull of a great ship
disappeared below the horizon. Falling off the
world's maps, he reached the vanishing point. He
was marooned in a salty drop of desire.

Flossing Shadows

The rain is warm: Jake's stacking boxes between
dresser and chairs in the rental truck, from scuffed
metal bed to dented ceiling, starting at the very back.
His shirt soon sticks to his chest, his sleeves have a
wet weight, matted hair streaks his forehead. Back
and forth along the sidewalk, he keeps bringing out
more. The rain rejuvenates him. He hefts blankets,
pillows, plates, books, fish kite, toolbox; he feels a
bobbing disembodiment in each step as he begins to
drift above the sidewalk. He empties the house until
the shadows left inside feel stripped and naked.

The porch light halos in the downfall darkness, air
glistening with fine droplets. Jake can't remember if
this is the third or fourth truckload. He's tired of
calculating how much is left, how much there is to go,
how to maneuver and squeeze in one more end table.
Who needs a leaky garden hose, a rusting can of rusty
screws? Leave the screws under the steps, leave the
hose snaking through the tall grass. With one last
brute shoulder shove, he closes the truck's rear doors.
He's moving into love.

Love Letter

Stella looks inside Jake's pillow case. There's an envelope instead of a flock of birds. No postage or cancellation, no address for delivery or return, but the glue on the flap has been licked and the letter sealed.

Standing beside the bed, she looks around the room. The chest of drawers is licked closed. The door to the room is licked closed. The blanket is licked smooth. She turns off the light to seal the mirror for the night.

Having to Ask

Shipwrecked, he's lying in bed wearing a torn work shirt, the covers pulled back. Jake's knees form two bony pink peaks in a mountain range that doesn't belong on this mattress and continues its synclines and anticlines somewhere else.

The slopes are cleared of trees and heavily terraced. Pencil-thin smoke from village fires scribbles up from deep gorges. Shrouded in clouds, a small herd of wild goats jump across the granite scree. The air in bed is fleshy.

The cat stretched along his left side purrs in his armpit. He's staring at the ceiling, waiting for a flat sky to lift. Last night's moon clings to the small west window.

He feels the ache of paths deeply rutted by oxcarts that lead to barley fields and the torrential rains that run along his thighs. None of this makes any difference.

He doesn't know anyone here. He doesn't know the language. He can't ask for the simplest thing. He lies back, pulls up the covers, and points to his open mouth.

Fire Slapstick

A fire races across his skin. His tears trail smoke. Off
the plains of Thermopylae updrafts fan the flames. A
rescue helicopter crashes into his face. Da Vinci-
drawn parachutes bloom across his forehead.

He hears the frantic bark of axes at work. Bulldozers
clear fire lines. It's too late. His charred stare frightens
the cats. Eyebrows smolder. Stepping into the shower,
he's a hissing ember choking on water. Steam billows
to the ceiling.

When he enters the third floor of the Aetna Building,
the receptionist wants to know what happened. He
can't remember a word of the argument, his fingers
blackened from holding too long to a lava flow.

A Very Cellular Birthday

Their young daughter Ismene says it's a stupid novel about time, and she's writing an even stupider report that will not be on time.

Stella doesn't think the novel is stupid but maybe time and space are the bad joke? It's what happens on cold nights when pieces of dying stars drive their fiery shanks through the sky. Shivering, Stella stares at the Milky Way, a sweep of sparkling ash, herself an aggregate of tired time congealing under a swayback eternity.

Graying locks, fingers like wrinkled keys, brittle bones, no hacksaw buried in the angel food cake, she occupies the space of a cell, her vision cataracted in the passing.

Sailing Thebes

Stella walks upstairs, sits in a stuffed blue chair. She
hears a shuffling so distant she can't quite make out
what it is or from what direction it's coming. It's the
whisper of a twenty-dollar bill taken from a wallet.
An old map razored from a book deep in the library
stacks. A hand-written note tucked in the pocket of a
passing stranger. She tilts her head to the left, to the
right. She's not sure what she's hearing. She rises
from the chair to get a glass of wine from the kitchen.

A few minutes later, Stella's back and so is the
susurrous slippage. She thinks it's the wind tugging
on the few winter leaves that haven't fallen from their
branches. Out the window everything is still. Not
even a half-starved squirrel jumps across the yard.
She looks a second time. There's the crinkling of
evening's lacquered light stretched to the breaking
point, but that's different.

She turns her head straining to hear something more.
Stella's glad there's no one in the room with her. This
could be the beginning of a diagnosis. To check her
hearing, she cups her hand, holds it over her ear. She
changes the curve of her fingers, hears a faint roaring,
it's the Aegean ebbing in her palms.

Vacuuming the Rich

Lately, the shadows in the rug bother her. She's spent
hours on her knees, straining to see shades of late
Klee in the fibers. Stella's convinced a masterpiece is
worn deep into the pile.

First she uses her fingers, but they're blunt
instruments. She finds the loose dirt, granules of
sand, specks of kitty litter. She resorts to tweezers and
a magnifying glass to separate the tissues of one
shadow from another. The operation is complicated,
delicate, too much light, too little light, and the
shadows are gone in glare, in gloom. She has a
conservator's patience, a museum's desire.

She holds up a pole lamp's thinning intimations. By
the end of the day, she's down to the carpet pad,
digging for aftershadows, Klee's real inspiration.
She's determined. The soles of sandaled senators the
only threat before she's finished vacuuming.

Attila at Breakfast

The milk carton she grabs from the refrigerator is
missing its pictures of missing children, as if everyone
is accounted: Joey still playing after a night in the
back yard, Reginald dodging yet another car
retrieving a fouled baseball, Sally a little too long in
her uncle's house, sure to burst from the front door
and head home soon. One whiff from the open carton
tells her the idle musings of a jersey has curdled.

She sits down to stare at the dry heap of broken and
twisted fibers of grain in her bowl. She sees what was
left of a village sacked and burned days ago. A hut
smolders. One cow remains, too skittish to give milk,
ready to run if fur-clad horsemen return. A gray
tabby leaps onto the table, hoping to lap up what's
left. Before she can say *shoo*, it bounds back to the
floor, not knowing what to do with a village of bones.
Stella's speechless.

Play It Again

It takes fifteen minutes for Jake's left foot to find the
pavement, fifteen more, give or take a few seconds,
for his right to lift and follow. He's taken a couple of
steps today. He's a drive-by target if someone shoots
at street poles.

Pickpockets miss him. They can't move that slow. He
ambulates as if there were no guilt to outdistance, no
appointments so late only last- minute sprints hold
hope, no deepening escape from his desperate life.

He'll make the corner drugstore by mid-afternoon.
Crowds race stoplights at the end of the block. He
thinks he's running as he's left behind. He holds up
an arrested universe and the police don't care.

Prestidigitation

Stella visits Delphi, North Carolina, on the Outer
Banks. A thief stole her camera from a bench while
she played Frisbee. So much for reading the
prophecies. She should have probed the goat entrails
a second time.

The trees won't tell her who, what, or when. Gnarled
branches point in all directions. She demands more
from the jays and sparrows. They squawk and twitter
away. She turns and quickly counts the first flowers.
Spring's still here.

Will the thief develop the film? Stella can't stand the
thought. Her friends, herself, laughter swarming the
couch, chasing the dog down the street, frame after
frame of smiles that a stranger will remember.

No Help

Stella's remembering the story that her parents never read to her, sitting in the small chair beside her bed where she lay, head sinking into a cloudy pillow, the book glowing in the light from the Hopalong Cassidy lampshade, pages flashing like the wings of a plane in moonlight. It's the one about the little Chinese boy who rides the wind. Actually, he's stolen a worn leather bag that's sealed tight, sewn closed with wet river reeds that dried in the sun and made the bag impossible to open, each stitch cinched deep into the leather. Of course, he doesn't listen to the warning of his elders. He takes a jade knife, green as spring pasture, and rips the side of the bag open.

The valley where the boy lived had been perfectly still for centuries, perhaps an eternity or two. Each leaf in its unmoving place; dust from the road always falling straight down. Now the trees are bending to the ground, their leaves spiraling around them like an aggravated hornet's nest. Peasants' hats sail off to sit on mountain peaks and become Taoist sages. Sparrows decide it's too dangerous to fly, drop from the eaves, and hop across gardens. The thatched village houses lose their roofs. The sky is crowded with cartwheeling straw. It's a festival. The boy is swept up, riding hard on the sweating back of wind. Over the horizon his face is in every cloud.

Today, leaning far back in a chair, she hears the boy moaning. There's a thin crack in the window frame where he's trying to get in. After all these years, he's grown tired of being blown here and there. But only the wind is thin enough to get through. She wraps its long thin threads onto a wooden spool to keep it from blowing papers off the desk. After the moans quiet down, she puts the spool into the sewing drawer. She will sew the boy a shirt of wind.

Concerted Effort

Ismene wrung the wah-wah pedaled, feedback-blasted notes out of her blouse and hair. She paused to pull up her mismatched socks, green and red, the mad dance that she panted through the evening with her boyfriend, Apollo. After the fourth encore, when the foot-stomping, hand-clapping, sweat-drenched crowd flagged, and the musicians had played through to the other side of their guitars, she chased after her bladder. Returning through the smoke and spilled beer, she hoped for one more chance to ride the music, but she was a full measure too late, red sock in the band's bus exhaust, green sock spinning on the dance floor.

Hearing Aid

Jake no longer wants to hear crickets hidden in
clumps of grass and under loose stones, the scrape of
their rough legs pacing the distance of a cold evening.
The mourning doves, too, perched in the arc of
telephone lines across a vaulted gray sky, cooing at
the edges of a perpetual grieving. Jake with two-inch
wide suspenders stretched across an ironed white
shirt, leans his head to the left to empty out one ear.
It's most of what he's heard: do this, do that, don't do
this or that, now and tomorrow, argumentative years,
skirmishes, border conflicts, stock market crashes,
depressions, recessions, the rumors that kept him
alive.

The room is too small for the chaotic, arbitrary,
inconsistent, random catalog that pours from the soft
shell of his convoluted flesh. He loosens his collar.
He's having trouble breathing, hearing again the
sighs, the cries, what once meant so much, now inert
at his feet. The Magna Carta and Hammarabi's Code
clink to the floor. There are bankruptcies and
divorces, all the legal accounting that kept his life a
disordered order. Beowulf and the Treaty of
Versailles lumps in the mounting rubble. The broken
guitar strings and drumsticks of Styx and Queen.
Walking to the other side of the windowless room, he
steps over calls-to-arms and inaugural addresses,
relieved not to listen anymore. His blood pressure
lowers, his short-trimmed beard grays, the skin on the
backs of his hands turns a papery translucence. When
the small bones of his ears are ready to tumble out
with an avalanche of ossified sounds, he is dissolving,

a mere shimmer of air. Another room to be closed and locked. Then Stella walks up to him, cups her small hands, and breathes into Jake's ear.

Wildlife in Thebes

Ungulated

Deer ate the peas, the most beautiful peas Stella had
grown in twenty years, if she can say she grew them
and that they didn't grow themselves, or that they
grew together, fingers fondling seeds into soiled
rows. Deer ate the fresh sweetness of her anticipation
along with the flat round leaves that stair-stepped up
the entwining vines to golden green pods. They ate
the enfolded white blossoms that Georgia O'Keefe
might have penetrated with her brushes. They left the
truncated, the decapitated, a fruitless, vined reaching.

The deer didn't stop. They nipped the frothing
magnificence of oregano, it's leafy slopes suggesting a
rugged perennial range now clipped back from
mountain to molehill. Gone the towering purple
blush of chives and the chrome-smooth tops of
pepper plants. The expansiveness of their palette, an
ungulatic haute cuisine.

But squash: the broad leaves and prickly stalks;
orange, loosely folded, napkin-sized flowers; the
finger-length zucchini; all eaten from the center out.
She drives metal posts with a sledge hammer,
aggravating her tennis elbow, flinching at the clang of
impact. She stretches costly five-feet-high, woven-
wire fencing. She ties rope from post to post, a
webbing above the plants, to discourage any leaps of
faith. She's digging in her hooves.

In the Trenches

Chunks of summer sky are falling. Heavy rain rocks
the tin roof. The house is buried in dripping rubble.
The cedar siding, sealed in oils from Guernica, keeps
both of them dry. Lightning sparks its heels across
drab clouds. Flamenco flashes all the way into
thunder. The chatter of castanets can be heard in hail
and loose windowpanes.

From his grave, Franco reaches up to grab what's left.
The geriatric Lincoln Brigade volunteers to clean its
closeted rifles. The storm dive bombs, the floor
shakes, light bulbs flicker, their only shelter chance.
They ache for another revolution of love. Stella & Jake
stand under the gutter spouts, naked before rain's
bayonets. They lick the wounded droplets from each
other's nipples.

Asymmetry

It's possible to describe the fingers and thumb as
more than opposable, as they work slowly around the
spaces between well-oiled toes, as if foot and fingers
go hand and hand on a stroll. Easing the toes back
into a position of pressure and pleasure, then rolling
each toe between finger and thumb so skin and
muscle slide over bone as if in love.

The palm downloads the heel's long day, polishes the
trophies of its velocities, and the thumb divines in the
arch's hidden arc . . . it's the details that Stella & Jake
cling to, that day to day tie together their lives . . . and
it is impossible not to mention lingering to knead
behind the knees, gliding along the calves, the slow
journey climbing the thighs with a gentle pulling
away of the feet as if being stretched toward another
world.

Night enters through the open window, wind sifts
through the lilac bush and screen, the cricket's steady
trill, and beyond, seeing the field stunned with
fireflies . . . there's the symmetry of hips, how the
fingers balance on the outriggers of bone, the
shoulders' sloping renunciation, the hand to hand
whispers, the pageant of the inner arm, the
anticipation . . . at night it's easy for Jake to believe in
discovery when it's really all invention. Stella says,
matter-of-factly, how much better it would be if she
didn't wake in the morning.

What Stella Doesn't Know About the Tailor

To pin down Ethereal, he runs the tape in and out a couple of times, listening to the snap of inches retreat into its metallic shell. It sounds alert. It sounds in control. It sounds professional.

Scissors rest on the table beside a rolled bolt of black velvet sky. Ready with paper and pencil to disclose the infinite, Jake hasn't forgotten the eraser. He expects to correct vast sums.

He feels his way along the skirt's hem. For more complex calculations, there's plumb bob and radio telescope, if Ethereal would just stand still.

For now, he has a waist measurement and knows her desire for a plunging neckline and low-cut back. Soon everyone in Thebes will recognize the elegant dresser walking the street, wearing a boutonniere laced with forget-me-nots, to Oblivion's house.

Betrayal

Jake stands by the table in the hall, shoulders drooping. He takes off his arms and legs, places them in the umbrella stand, hangs his torso beside the ragged coats, and buries his head on the shelf in an avalanche of hats. What's left of the day, what's left to walk down the hall, past the dusty portraits and dull landscapes hanging on the walls, but his dismemberment.

It's then he notices the square plastic CD cover placed on top of a folded blouse. It's one he impulsively bought a few years ago while on vacation in a small mountain town. The band on the sidewalk in front of the courthouse, far from their own country, played bamboo panpipes and cane flutes, the charango fashioned from armadillo shells, deer-skin drums, a large bambos. What he heard in the rattle of ribboned goat-hoof clippings was wind and rain cascading down rocky slopes.

Jake was drawn to their rhythms, certainly not to dance, he was not a dancer, but he could feel his bones being released from his flesh. He was trapped in webbing harmonies, could not move until the evening turned solidly night. Lured, snared, a victim uplifted to the peaked silhouettes still visible in the western sky, blown by the breath of musicians through insistent, staccato notes, flutes brimming and empty as wild mountain valleys, he found himself breathlessly running precipitous paths through scudding clouds until they finished their last song and rolled their instruments into colorful woolen blankets. It was at that moment before the band headed for the next tourist town that he bought the CD. Under the street lamp, he was left holding a small plastic box.

In the dim kitchen, the odor of garlic and onions crowding the corners, steam forming tears and sweating on the glassed portraits of aunts and uncles hanging around the table, when asked why the CD is by the door, Stella says she couldn't remember the name of the instrument, the one made of many small woven-together bamboo reeds, each one shorter than the last.

Endearments

Monday at work, Jake was called a *dirty bastard*, lovingly of course, when he stuck a cold Coke can, fresh from the vending machine, down the t-shirt of the man who runs the distribution department. The man arched his back, leaped into the air like a just-hooked bass breaking the surface of a farm pond. Some days Jake is too much rowing his own boat.

Tuesday Jake was called just a plain *butthead*, lovingly of course, when he stole the receptionist's camera from her desk. He took pictures of her sitting behind the counter, reading yet another romance novel, *The Hellion Bride*. He returned the camera. Wait till she develops the film and finds out what else is there.

Wednesday Jake was lovingly called a *turkey butt* as he was jogging the wide aisles of the warehouse at the end of the day, when a stocker with her coat on, intent on quitting time and the rear door, didn't hear his heavy breathing and the heel-toe pounding of his tired heart. He came up from behind, lightly jabbed her in the ribs with his index fingers, and startled her cry for revenge.

What to expect Thursday? He doesn't know. He just turned the lights on in his office, lovingly, of course. He's taking Friday off.

Dated

Jake missed the season's first storm and stood around
in a short-sleeved shirt on Thanksgiving, out of place
for more than weathered reasons. New Year's Eve,
preceded by two days of sun, kept its regular
appointment. By the time revelers considered
recovering another year, the sleet was covered by
snow and morning.

Sun arcs off surrounding fields, the light deafening.
Every unnoticed detail in the room is too loud. Dust
swirls over shelves where so much is still unread. All
this light doesn't help, when Stella asks, "Where's the
new calendar?" He walks into the next room and
can't remember, can't imagine where it is. Not under
any recent stacks of books growing up from the floor
like a subterranean city skyline.

Still hanging on the wall, the old calendar grows light
with all its day's crossed out.   December's
photograph: sandstone darkened by desert patina, the
chiseled outline of a hunter, bow raised, arm bent as if
he'd just released an arrow. His petroglyphic prey
runs in a millennium long chase down stone, across
the room and up the sheet-rocked wall, threatened
not by weathering, lichen, acid rain, graffiti, but a
new year of old French Impressionists.

The year's hunt over. The new calendar hangs behind
the old. The old year ready to be skinned. Stella &

Jake can begin the January countdown with a tribe on a distant river bank watching *A Bather at Asnieres*.

Extasy

Jake looks like anyone else who has driven onto acres of pavement and parked between Chevy and Ford, between rust and dent, between cracked windshield and bald tire, between screaming kids and screaming at them, between honked horn and slammed door, between diagonal white line and diagonal white line, between overturned shopping carts and empty blue plastic bags bristling like dogs as they inflate in the wakes of passing customers. He wants something to break its leash and run. He can't with the windows wound up and the air conditioner broken. The sun heaves its full weight onto his face and chest, holds him down, places its burning hand next to his on the torn seat. He's fried, and if he could shout, who would hear him, who would dare join a party of psychics to search this overheated realm warping and seething over August asphalt?

His flesh glazed with an exuberant sweat, the inside of the car a Turkish bath, windows steamed with his own sizzling essence. Shrouded in dust, the car begins to rock. He bends forward to pick a rag off the floor and smears the glass for a better view of swaying lampposts. A confetti of trash blows wildly across the pavement. Shoppers walking toward their cars begin to lean in acute directions. They have trouble placing the foot of their next step down. They tumble backwards dodging body-sized black letters blown off a movie marquee. An avenging alphabet clubs people with "T's" and "A's ", lassoing one woman with a capital "O". He sees a pickup shiver, the van next to it buck, and both somersault simultaneously, landing on crushed roofs. The parking lot's a croupier's table. The wind closes all bets. More cars are turned over and grind across the asphalt. Undercarriage, exhaust pipe, transmissions indecently exposed. He remains seated, his hands are solid, hot, clinging to the motionless steering wheel.

Light flames every window. His timing directionless, he begins to worry about the future of his past. He's young, he's old; in love, not in love; leaving for Salzburg, Austria, living in Rocheport, Missouri; a theory of relativity and a belief in an absolute dissolution. Disorder: a tornado of paper cups and plastic bags, new swing sets shuddering in maniacal arcs, lawnmowers banging against cinder block walls. He grabs for the door handle, shoves rusty hinges open, braces himself, steps out, expects to be stripped of his skin, but the sun is behind a cloud and the breeze barely touches the planter geranium's red petals. He hears the thrumming of nearby traffic, a meadowlark's song in a field staked with orange ribbons, a bulldozer starting its diesel. Einstein was wrong about dice and the universe. It's black jack as the dozer drops its shiny blade.

Obnubliation

Mirrored morning over the bathroom sink, he lifts Occam's Razor to his chin, finely slicing away the obtuse, the superfluous, the irrational stubble that grew overnight. Jake stares into the face of years and shapes the white lather into a goatee. He raises his right hand, as if to pontificate, and probes the steamy showered air for something to say.

He stares into his clean-shaven face, wondering who it was twenty years ago, bearded, who stood beside a barn late into the night, captivated by a monstrous thunderhead rearing high over the southern horizon. Rising through the immensity, star-swarms surrounded by strobed lightning, bolts breeching the cumulus' distended sides, firing an incessant magnesium throb, unraveling titanium nerves. Shadows of trees and fence posts shivered. As he swatted a mosquito, his hand disappeared three times in the disgorging light; and not a sound, the August crickets and whip-poor-wills stricken mute.

Attracted, repelled, tired, he returned to the house. It happened then, from ridges and valleys away, through explosions of light and dark, a wail thin as a needle pierced the stillness. It threaded its way toward him, growing louder, as if he were the only one awake to hear it, as if he were its destination. Over oaks, across mown fields, dusty roads, into the yard, the wail homed and circled the house, never touching the ground, shaking the window panes,

unnerving the rooms, singeing the hair of his scalp,
and then spun away. He rushed the door, raced
outside, saw nothing but night's skin pulled tight as
a drumhead thumping with light.

Jake runs his hand over his face, feels a roughness
he's missed. In the mirror, he aims an upward stroke
of the razor along his neck, beside his Adam's apple,
and nicks himself. A burning sensation; a blood
bead forms quick as lightning. Tearing a corner of
tissue, he places it on the cut; it flushes red, a
carnation clinging to his throat, a simple explanation.

Theban Ruins

The lamp is dim, the night narrow. What illuminates
the book is old and frayed, crumbling at the edges,
the ruins of reading.

Her lap weighted with a yellow dust. Booted
footnotes leave prints over her thighs, armies of
scholars on the march. Through late ashes, she is a
fading ember.

The plot is thin, weak. Gruel spooned into stricken
mouths. Conclusions to hate, greed, desperation,
exhausted logic, seasoned with the soup of bodies
boiling in ditches.

A Maginot Line, a Chamberlain. Nothing to stop it
from happening, nothing to stop her from falling into
a deathly sleep.

Her eyes are watery from strain. Her glasses
streaked, askew. Stella stares into and out of the dark
grass she's growing into.

Amputee

Jake has more jobs than fingers and at least one job
he'd like to cut off. He dreams to be left alone in the
garage enhancing the perpetual motion machine that
he's become, racing from counseling to jogging to
philosophy lecture, simultaneously answering phone
calls and letters as he sits at his desk in a windowless
room ripe with old car grease. But really, today's job
requires little preparation. He knows it's always and
only a matter of time. He makes plans, the rent past
due, the chasm of debt always gaping wider, it's just
one more paycheck.

The day a flawless blue, a soul staring up too long is
convinced, becomes dizzy, and tumbles into the sky.
A shivering wake, the dry leaves shouldering the
road as the procession of sober-colored cars pass,
passing plastic flowers, wilted flags, three dogs by the
stone gate, the child in a far yard bouncing a ball. All
become still, so still they slow the lead limousine until
it stops, separating space from time. On cloudy days,
souls walk off into a mist that leaves the suited
grievers in their own moist little bowls, surrounded
by polished granite tablets. The crowning oaks reach
out to pull them in the direction they need to go. On
windy afternoons, the mourners are anchored by their
downturned heads, their billowing coats the rotting
sails of beached schooners.

It's so easy, how each moment, in the loosening of
time, of space, turns sacred, falls effortlessly into

55

place, dust to dust, down to the backhoe that's out of
sight. But Jake has so many jobs, so many
commitments, he's a particle in a linear accelerator.
There are days he's close to colliding with himself,
close to splitting into something smaller before
mushrooming out of control. He needs a vacation.
Not a Caribbean cruise, not a phoneless motel room
outside the city with infinite cable channels, not a trip
to Texarkana. He's got to get away. This is the job that
he hates most. On blue, wind-struck days, in
cemeteries, Jake vacations with death, standing under
miles of sky delivering apocryphal tales over Thebans
he's never known.

Blue Migration

Jake's in some kind of too late mid-life crisis, not that
he thinks in those terms, though he's consumed by a
feeling of unease, really a subtle and growing disease,
whose diagnosis is not obvious to any of his friends,
or health care workers, two types he's strenuously
avoided these last months. It could quickly turn
deadly, not that there was really any hopeful
prognosis, and too easily, cynically, summed up
behind his back by "sooner or later."

He turns into the satellite bank's parking lot, the
afternoon a perfection of blue—there's nothing to see
with his head tilted back into a falling-up sky. On
days like this, emergency rooms are crowded with a
rush of vertigo cases: sand grains blown off the
beaches of patients' inner ears, all who want to leave
the planet, be transported, seduced into the infinite,
eternal, ethereal, out-of-body, out-of-mind, out-of-
this-stinking-place, head-for-the-hills, head-for-the-
stars, take-the-money-and-run . . . wait he's stopped,
the only dented, wheel-well rusted, right rear-
taillight-missing, no hub caps, car in the lot, that looks
half like an abandoned osprey nest. When he opens
the door, he's taking flight, moving out onto a limb of
sidewalk, and he almost raises his arms to begin
flapping.

Jake enters through the double-tinted glass doors,
hands in his pockets, there to check his balance, walk
the tightrope of accounting, slip past the noose of
overdrafts, make a small deposit. The silent TV

mounted in one ceiling corner displays the enclosed captions of CNN. Morning's stale coffee sits in a silver urn beside the stacked peak of Styrofoam cups. A bowl of Jolly Rogers by the only open teller's window, and in her practiced, mellifluous voice she says, "How can I help you?" and he can't remember, he's a fledgling falling from a nest, a jettisoned rocket booster tumbling through space, an aging man in a too quickly aging moment.

She asks again, and rather than opening his wallet and signing the check, he says in a meek monotone, "Give me all your money," and pulling off his sweat-stained baseball cap to use as a pathetic receptacle, the teller dutifully, awkwardly stuffs the hat and hands it back. He flies out as slowly as he walked in. He's sitting in the car, staring up through the dirty windshield at a single stringy cloud that's cracked the sky, when three police cars careen past, lights flashing. They run into the bank, guns drawn.

Having completed their reports, dusted for fingerprints, reviewed the video cameras, they have no leads. Jake's still nesting in his car when the police leave the bank. It's not clear to him, the money spilled across the passenger seat, wrapped in small bundles like green dominoes, if he's dead or just the soul of a bird in flight.

How Tables Learn to Talk

Jake can tell you what and maybe why he pulled back
the covers and got up, sitting for a moment on the
edge of the bed, taking one conscious breath then
another, inflating the body back to life, left hand
feeling for glasses on the night stand, chin on chest
keeping his head from falling to the floor.

It was around 2 a.m. when the table startled itself
awake, realizing it was no longer in the kitchen and
hadn't been for hours. With wooden legs and a
lumbering Frankenstein gait, it must have
sleepwalked into the living room. Paralyzed with
fear, it couldn't make it back to surround itself with
chairs and so became a ventriloquist, shouting
through the woman standing next to it, Stella in a
night shirt and naked from the waist down.

It must be moved now, not before breakfast, not after
showering, not before leaving for work, but now in
the moonlight slipping across the newly waxed floor,
dry with shadows. Tables are so hysterical when they
wake in the wrong room.

Theban Timing

Hardly a whisper of light at the window. Claws
slowly rake the glass. The black cat that sits on the sill
has already heard it and wants out, but isn't ready to
pounce on the deafly sleeping couple in bed.

The radio alarm begins to rattle loose news:
explosions, corruptions, insurrections, floods, houses
burglared and burned, the dead mounting every
barricade.

Jake threads his way through five cats stretched over
the blankets. He's thinking Monday after the first
weekend in November and he forgot to reset the
clocks to daylight savings time.

Stella wriggles her way through the same crowd of
cats, but counts seven overweight purring bodies.
Sums unrequited, they both realize they are late or
early for work.

Jake hurries upstairs to change the pink digital clock
in the study, abandoned by their daughter when she
outgrew the color and left for college.

Stella quick to the kitchen to reset the stove clock, and
the one that hangs over the kitchen table, a childhood
relic, a wooden owl whose eyes stopped counting the
seconds long ago and now stare in one exaggerated

direction, its heart stuffed with gears.

Downstairs, Stella spins the clock's arms an hour
ahead. Upstairs, Jake draws them back an hour. Two
hours apart, they've lived in this house for thirty
years.

Theban Planet

The unmatched pair of shoes next to Jake's side of the bed claim a glorious lineage. The right shoe belongs to General Douglas MacArthur and keeps saying, "I shall return," as it walks off toward the underside of the foundation springs. The left one was worn by Khrushchev and bangs on the worn oak floor, demanding negotiations while proclaiming burial rights. All night he lies awake dealing with international crises and Stella still won't roll over and talk to him.

Theban Traffic

Résumé

Each pothole has a face. She stops on the gravel
shoulder, steps out of the car into traffic, bends over,
looks down, oblivious to the horns of swerving
oblivion. She stares harder and is nearly run over.

Late winters are especially busy. There are so many
breaking open, so many to welcome back. She looks
past the concrete's crumbling edges, the spidering
cracks, to what has collapsed inward: jaw, eyebrow,
sinuses, casualties of the latest undeclared war.

Stella wants them to know they are not alone. There
are secret gaps in everyone's résumé. For days, the
holes are flooded with rain and slush. What stares
back scares her. She says she's there to help, even as
she turns her back, covering her head as another car
speeds past, the splash titanic, the stranger's
alignment ruined.

Sphinx

Five o'clock: shaggy vapored horizon, scalloped
clouds step down the sky, sun-blind gleam through
the cubist geometry of far buildings.

Stella turns from the parking lot onto the secondary
road. At the intersection, a semi blocks the freeway
entrance, poised to make a wide right turn no matter
what.

She needs to swing into the center lane if she's to turn
left across the opposite flow of traffic. She pulls
around the stopped car in front of her.

She accelerates as the path clears. A rusted, fifties
vintage, high-finned Ford races past. Both cars forced
to swerve, she drives her foot down hard on the
brakes as books and mail reshuffle over the dirty
floor.

She doesn't know who's the riddle and who's the
answer. She swears there was nothing coming. She
swears as she crawls through traffic.

Hurdling Epic

First in class, first in line anywhere for anything, first
to run the edges of destruction, Stella craved the high-
school spotlight. She stood on the shoulder of a six-
lane highway, midnight, late February, wind winter-
brittle, her right arm and thumb extended, her hair
caught in a gust, obscuring her movie-glitter eyes. She
was captured in the sweep of headlights, hearing the
many engines' accelerating applause.

There's the chance she might for one night have
stopped her own careening, her own swerve and
crash, as headlights began to shatter at her edges. She
had a plan. She never had a plan. She repeated the
mantra with each second of flashing fame, her black
hair trailing off tangled far into night's ebbing
asphalt, her most dramatic in and out of town until
she collided with Jake.

Executing Fireflies

By the time Stella and Jake even wonder about it, they've wandered too far onto the next road, into the next house, town, pasture, too far to recall details: where, when, how, above, behind, all that creeps up that is suddenly there and gone like the blinking of fireflies perforating moist night fields. They forget how to follow the illuminated instructions for tearing here and here. When they do unscrew the lids and open their jarred darknesses, the rules are broken, the vagueness of their lives pulsating and monumental, and they can't recall how to connect the rhythmic, flashing dots to form a line of flight.

Those Things

Jake preparing to talk to his son, remembers his father
in the hospital bed, slowly entangled and lost amid a
maze of tubes, and when from a chair by the window
he asked if there was anything his father regretted, he
answered, "I'd go to the temple more often and I'd
have talked to you about those things."

With long strokes that bent Jake's body like an
oarsman, he massaged his father's swollen calves.
They'd never touched except to shake hands, and
only once did Jake cry to his father's face, when he
accused him of not caring, when he was young and
still cared, but in those last months, when flowers
lined the window sills and Jake read to him, they held
hands.

Jake never saw his father naked, and he hasn't seen
his son naked in years, though he knows his young
body is being driven to collide with others. Yesterday
on the basketball court, when his son raised his arms
to shoot, he saw dark tangles of hair.

He wonders what more it was his father had wanted
to tell him that evening just after he'd learned to
drive, when he walked over to the Volkswagen. Jake
started the engine as his father leaned toward the
window, as if to whisper. Though no one was near,
his hand covered the side mirror when he said,
"Protect yourself." That was it and Jake backed out of
the driveway.

Results & Prospects in Thebes

Trotsky said, "The biggest surprise that comes to a man is old age," or something like that, and Jake's hurting back and stiff left knee know. Leader of the October Revolution, Trotsky knew how it ends at the barricades, one more body to add to the heap. Sooner or later, say in a sidewalk café in Trieste, sharing coffee and scones, the early hours uneventful and lacking imagination, the proletariat rushing to work, he would meet with his bullet, or in New York City, a car would swerve at a busy intersection, taking in his whole body, dragging him half a block before speeding off, or at last at his house in Coyoacán, ice-picked by a Spanish Stalinist. No accident of aim, the bloody sickle-flapping full-faced.

Or was he saying that the wizened old man sitting on the eroding lip of the plaza fountain, his face wrinkled with light, battered fedora shading his eyes, his clichéd pose, chin on top of both hands, cupped over a wooden cane, half-dreaming of his half-heroics, having not fallen at the palace gates, now half-dozing to the water streaming from the open mouths of concrete nymphs behind him and the cooing of pigeons in the Church of Guadalupe bell tower, that this is the lost last revolution, and Jake despairs from both sides of the argument.

Theban Diaries

Stella can smell it though the curtains are pulled
closed and the bedroom door shut. There's no room
on the table with stacks of newspaper headlines
declaring Kennedy assassinated, Nixon resigning, the
war over, the war lost, the next war to be better.

It's not because what smells vaguely unappetizing is
shoved under the couch, that space overpopulated
long ago with shoes that wandered there. There's so
much of everything misplaced and longed for.

Still the accumulation on the dresser is historic and
historical. Jake, the beast over his plate of sausage and
kraut, eats out of a chest of drawers, slamming it shut
if Stella enters the room. Not another bite until she
leaves. She can't watch him eat another of his words.

Hanging Gardens of Thebes

Men with flowery hands who planted themselves in
mine shafts, assembly lines, wars, plow their own
flesh. She watches them work gardens that grow
slowly wild, where they disappear under a row of
gardenias, behind sunflowers, or trellised morning
glories, or just bury themselves deep in soiled
pockets. She finds their vines growing in closets,
hanging from clothes poles like tired snakes just
wanting to coil around another hour of dark rest.

In basements too, they uproot concrete and tile floors,
their work so conscientious their lives turn a rich
moist green. When discovered, they surrender to her
and she weeds their shrugging shoulders.

Don't forget attics, where mummified details are
arranged in bouquets that hang bat-like from rafters
beside yellowing photographs and uniforms. Always
a few prized petals pressed between pages of cracked
leather-bound centuries that recall the hands that
placed them there.

Theban Cacophony

He sits with the wooden body in his lap. His right
arm is gently wrapped around one surface of the
immaculate varnish. The curves sweep inward from
both sides—an empire waist. From one angle it is
pear-shaped. From another undeniably that of a
voluptuous woman. From a third it's an endless
celloed embrace. Facing full-frontal, it is naked,
immodestly covered by a few taut strings.

To the symbolist it is an armless stick figure
communicating the plight of humans, strumming
their pathetic condition. To the cymbalist only a
rhythmic wooden ringing makes sense, beating the
hollowed body into submission. To the spiritualist it
is the soul's hoe working row after row of the staff.

Jake's left hand slides up and down the polished
neck. He can feel the pulse of wood. His hand glides
then takes flight. His hand is leaving his body to join
the stratospheric score. His hand circles above
waving. It will not return for minutes, and upon
landing his fingers are a raucous flock of ravens
perched on each string, ravaging the notes.

Middle Way

Is it possible to believe that one can have a god
without using him?

—R. M. Rilke

Roadside histories of these caffeinated high-plains
miles are footnoted in the dirty punctuation of
discarded Styrofoam cups, ranchers' battered baseball
hats displaying Hermes' winged herbicide logos as
they take flight across the median, wind-inflated
plastic bags lurching through sparse grass, and blown
retreads peeling off into blinding distances. He once
stood in the middle of this vast horizon at the edge of
glistening noonday concrete, thumbing through the
wake of the occasional passing car. Headed east, he
kicked up dust and anthills. Headed west, he doubled
back to watch pronghorn antelope graze sagebrush.

Hours with the weight of days dulled his decision. He
threw his backpack onto the bed of the first pickup
that stopped. Turning off the highway onto a gravel
road, another pickup pulled in behind them. He
wanted to metamorphose into the caterpillar of dust
billowing behind the truck, but they drove too fast
toward the edge of the world to leap into flight.

Stopped at the intersection of nothing and nowhere,
big-buckled, cowboy-booted young men surrounded
him. The steel blades of drawn buck knives sliced thin

acetylene slivers of light. Shoved to the ground, he knelt as they hacked at his long hair. Done, his head looked like any of those desiccated low hills, a few scattered creosote shrubs with trickles of blood meandering among overheated rocks. Shoved farther into the dirt, they unzipped their jeans and a half-dozen yellow streams anointed his shorn scalp. Pack on the ground, he was left to find his own way back.

Enlightenment Again

Boards begin to fall from the bedroom walls spilling
mummified masses, ratty nests and fragile toothpick
skeletons. Wasps released, fly into his gaping mouth.
He's sure he's not speaking as words buzz around his
face. He swings once at the air then punches his fist
through the wall. He looks into the hole. It's a cave on
a steep mountain slope above the tree line where he
has lived a thousand years. Stepping back, he sees
that the wall is covered with caves.

Sand Locust

When the seventeen- and eleven-year locust cycle
crossed in August, the air hummed through the day
and far into the evening. Heat shimmered to their
pitch. The hairs on Jake's arm were thousands of
tuning forks. He was an instrument played by a
plague of insects. Nothing was immune. Distant
traffic harmonized. He was hearing them from the
inside out. At any moment, he might have crawled
out of his human husk and flown up into a tree.

A monk rubs a ribbed metal funnel with a wooden
stick. The vibration cascades colored sand in a needle-
thin stream. He lays the last few frills to complete the
circumference. A canary-yellow perches on a parrot-
green background. It's taken five days to fly out from
the center of a five-foot circle. The steel funnel a locust
wakened by rubbing. Days the room trembled to the
steady trill.

Monastery

In long rows, six-legged monks walk down damp-
shadowed walls, arriving from the attic where they've
spent long months sequestered in low-raftered winter
meditation. The lines diverge, head for the sink, the
stove, the cat food bowl. Tiny Buddhas come not to
pick the bones of the body clean, but to clamp their
vice-like mandibles onto the more subtle, more
painful realms of survival. They gather in mandala-
like circles around the drops of clear poison dripped
on the floor, their black heads pressed together
nurturing their impermanence.

Trouble with the Egyptian Travel Agent

1

The mullahs in their needle-thin towers call prayers
out of the shriveled earth. All Jake wants is to forget.
The room's curtains buckle in hot winds. This
morning he smells the aromas of bitter coffee. On the
floor below, Oasis Café patrons empty their thickly
brewed cups. He runs his tongue over the crushed
blood of his shattered lips. By noon the heat builds its
own ephemeral city, scooping the heaped odors of the
living to the second story. Later the shadows of
windows, of date palms, of dusty white-washed
buildings, are awash in a lacquered light. He can no
longer be certain what city this is. Time and joy have
betrayed him. He doesn't care to see, even if he could
raise a swollen eyelid, the window welded to light
and the empty heat-stricken streets. He chokes on
stale sweat mixing with the new efforts of his
interrogators to once again beat their truth into him,
the fact of their fists clear, his identity less so. What is
written on the mattress, his clothes, the floor, are facts
he cannot betray. This has gone on so long even the
man who only whispers raises his voice and the other
man who has said nothing begins to crack sore
knuckles. Jake grows lighter than the arguments of
his life. Floating near the swan-shaped blades of the
ancient ceiling fan, he is swept out the window, an
enlightened wisp. The interrogators jump to catch
hold of his foot, truth quickly out of reach high above
the street.

2

Leaning out the window, enjoying the cool evening
breeze, watching it ripple palm fronds, stir the
embroidered light and shadows that spread over the
town, two men light each other's cigarettes, the
smoke trailing from their lips as if a plane or a
prophet had crashed somewhere deep in their sun-
scarred, eroded faces. Thousands of years have gone
into the perfection of their profession, the secret
societies of power that covet occult knowledge and
unremitting repression. They are relaxed yet know
they have failed. A travel agent's mistake when
Thebes is not Thebes, still someone has escaped them
and lies limp on the floor. They must decide what to
do. Should they report this incident to their superior,
admit their failure? Should they deny they ever found
their victim wandering the bazaar? Is not the truth
more important than the petty details that lead from
room to room, from town to casbah, from one
nameless dune to another, from one life to the other?
In one whisper they have loaded the body into a jeep.
It is a good night to drive the desert. They know their
destination. They have paid their respects to its
anonymity many times. In daylight it can be located
by the ever-reforming question mark of slow circling
birds and at night by the jackals' yawp. They return to
town early in the morning, lightened by the dumping
of a failed body of truth.

3

Far into the desert, dunes quiver in the after-heat,
inviting any man to lie down with them in a star-
stunned night. It's the morning chill that awakens
Jake. The warmth radiating from the sand as the cold
air presses down, confuses his body and obscures the
pain. He's still as the rocks in *Wadi el Hôl*. He rolls his
head to one side, eyes puffy distortions, and sees the
desert beginning to discover its shadows. He can't
remember his arrival. His condition, that of a bruised
fruit carried too many caravaned miles, dropped from
a saddlebag and trampled by each passing hour. He's
become a memory beyond remembering. He must
find a beginning in this dry place or he will exist here
forever. He recalls being tied into a laundry bag,
flung into the back of an ancient vehicle whose engine
hacked and coughed its way out of town. He was
driven hours, dumped at the foot of these side-
slipping dunes. Stones knuckle into his bleeding back.
Or is this the wrong beginning as it must be when
Thebes is not his Thebes? Should he look for a
smudge of smoke and the wreckage of a 747? Surely,
this would better explain his ripped lips, his swollen
hands, his purpled chest, and twisted legs. The wind
hisses over the sand. His only companions are fist-
sized scorpions crawling near him. Jake offers his
open palms.

4

In the room there is a lateness to each hour. Each
minute falls, as if there is nothing so distant as a
minute ago. Walls exchange austere colors with the
passing of day. The ceiling fan a metronome of
uncertainty, tilts toward cruel conclusions as earth
wobbles toward its own seasonal demise. Anymore,
he rarely gets up from his desk to stretch his legs,
walk to the window. He knows his domain is wider
than any city or village in this deserted country. It's
subterranean and deeper. Thousands of years are
resurrected in shadows. The obelisks dive into their
needled darknesses. Hawk-headed men walk past his
window. Baboons scratch at his door. An ibis perches
on the balcony. Karnak's crumbling colonnade breaks
into immeasurable angles of Luxor. The sun is
enthroned on the Avenue of Sphinxes. He has probed
living flesh and found it wanting. He picks up the
glass, leaving a moist ring on the papers stacked
beside the telephone. The melting ice cubes are
windows to that other world he seeks. The sweating
glass meets his sweaty lips and he gulps down sash,
sill, and pane. He sees the entire town with one
glance: the narrow streets and squat houses, palms
and minarets, awash in a burning river of light.
There's knocking at his door, slow and dusty as if an
ancient temple were collapsing. He already knows of
their failure. He is not a cruel man. He will let them
fail again. He knows the world is truth in the shape of
a lie.

5

Days, weeks, Jake no longer can tell the length of his
own story. It did not end as others declared. In town
few dared to whisper of this accidental tourist's
absence. Fingers point at the hole on the street corner
where he once stood, in the café where he drank
coffee waiting for his travel agent to return his call.
His truth is the inadvertent lapse in the great scheme
between dawn and dusk of an empire of heat and
shadows. When he reaches the well at the edge of
town, where the women gather to fill their buckets,
bruises are no longer visible on his arms, lips are
again a continuous line of scarred words. One eye
focuses on the finest details of the present: the
thirteen flies that plague the ass tied to a date tree, the
thirteen lice on the baker's head, the shrill voices of
thirteen locusts squaring thirteen behind the stable.
The other eye stares off into a distance deeper than
ruin. There is an unsettling grace in his twisted face.
He has returned with no gifts, no stone tablets, no
hope of salvation. Before he sets out for his other
Thebes, it's simple what he says to anyone who asks:
*We suffer the tortured amazement of each day. The desert
must be crossed.*

Terrorist in Thebes

Candles of various heights stand like the thin towers
of an evening city. He strikes a match to light the
dozen that sit on the table in the yard. Their high-
storied windows begin to melt. He places a candle in
each of the empty wine bottles that await their new
renters. He sticks a candle in his mouth, his tongue a
prophetic sputter.

Constellations of Christmas lights arc through low
cedar branches. Dusk suspended in ashen clouds.
Stars begin to shimmer in his wine glass: Canis Major,
Sirius, the black hole of alcohol sucking in their light.
What an easy strangeness uncharted between broom
and dustpan, between himself and the woman across
the table. He looks down at the flickering city
avenues. He looks down at the broom and dustpan, at
himself and the woman across the table. He is a minor
gaudy god. A wax river drips off the table and
congeals in the dirt. Star cities mix and burn together.

Invention of Thebes

Nicked Name

Reinventing the pretzel as a tool of assassination, one
heel propped on a fire hydrant, spine bent forward,
hand reaching for his toes, he's stretching before
jogging. He notices the sewer grate, the wrist-thick,
rusting iron lattice and the dark brick-sized vacant
rectangles that are passages for what is to pass
through and beyond.

The voids remind him of bricks sealed between wide
runs of reddish mortar. He sees behind the flattened
walls to the people living flat lives. Standing, they lie
on their sides. Lying down to sleep, they stand. To
move from kitchen to bedroom, they roll, as if life is
always on the downhill side of Sisyphus. Is it a
coincidence that Jake's nickname is Jack and Stella's is
Jill. Jack's invested heavily in Advil, he's a
pharmaceutical sales rep. Jill's forever about to dial
911.

What kind of life is it rolling all day between
headache and emergency? On this street, they are just
a wall away from cigarette butts, paper cups,
newspaper blankets and cardboard houses, the
accumulated grime of a world flooding out of
existence with the next rain And the next will bring it
all back. The street light changes and Jake continues
to jog down someone's wall.

Just Right

Mid-November, stars a madness of unknowable
references—not that there aren't enough other
reasons for Jake to relinquish his sanity: painting the
house and not knowing that he isn't supposed to be
painting the house, an oil-based cover-up of
accusations for all the other lives he hasn't lived; the
car dead and a new battery unable to move seized
pistons; swinging eight pounds of sharpened steel
over his shoulder to split firewood and finding
Robespierre's red deep in the grain; or how to be sure
that the papyrus pulled from an Egyptian crocodile
mummy contains unknown poems by Posidippus
from the court of Ptolemy II Phildelphus and not by
the greater poet Callimachus.

Jake leans back knowing that this sweep of star
splendor is the product of astronomy's *Goldilocks'
Dilemma,* that immeasurable subatomic moment after
the Big Bang when a too dense universe would have
immediately collapsed into a black hole, ending it all
before much of anything got started, or a too light
universe that would have just blown away before
forming a single cosmic body—results the same.

How easily a young girl with blond pigtails dressed
in flowery dirndl at that big-banged moment, before
pigtails and dirndls, might find a swirl of purple or
red or bruised orange, before there were colors or
playground bruises, just unfathomable, imperceptible
wavelengths, and she might be attracted to and think

this is worth keeping and want to place it in her apron pocket, before there were any thoughts and wants and aprons, and when she sits down to three bowls, the porridge in one too heavy, the next too light, and the last just right, and it's the last that she spoons up, even though it's a lumpy cold universe, and then she naps, not in the too hard, not in the too soft, but in the just right bed, dreaming something ever-expanding out the window, not too fast or too slow that might abandon her but something that will wait for her to evolve, all before windows and dreams, then startled awake she runs frightened out the door, when the three furry nothings trundle in, Mama, Papa, and Baby, to chase that thieving street urchin Goldilocks, leaving a trail of nebula and galaxies to follow back to their just right beginnings, which is mostly what we search for, the just right, and go mad or are exhausted never finding it. Even if Jake does paint the house, get the car running, cut enough wood to stay warm through another wobble of the planet, and ponder 2,500-year-old lines of doggerel— it can't be anything less than just right.

Thebedom Pigdom

Stella has to dodge chic fiberglass. These city-sponsored artsy pigs are on every street corner where she shops. A very pink one in green sock hat and matching knitted sweater stands in seventy degree weather, wearing two pairs of skis, and squeals all day. Too hot for snow on a dry hill, the pig drags a concrete wake.

In the plaza, there's a pig pair beside a stainless steel Ionic column that's chopped into its own ruins like a pile of severed fingers. Pigs can't begin to grasp this seismic dislocation, and could care less, they're just looking for an ontologic mud hole. They want to discuss the swill of sewers, murky gutters, because that's all there is while waiting for the uptown bus.

In the market, dead fish sail through the air to the cash register. A pig leans against the wharf railing, pole suspended over the ferry-chopped water. Covered in scales, she might be mistaken for a fat dragon. Pig snout plus porpoise-finned back says otherwise. No corkscrew tail but a wiggly-fish thing. The porcine maid reflects on the pigmutations of these busy streets as Stella rides sardined in the downtown trolley.

Say Anything Theban

Lips left on the elevator talking to a beautiful
stranger. How much they yearn to return to that last
awkward sentence, correct it, smooth out the stutter,
say more, but they're gone, fallen into a pocket,
caught on a key chain, dangling in a stranger's half-
turned door lock.

Waxing Ubermensch

Column of yellowed wax, wick exposed a quarter inch, begging a match—she knows where there's a book in the back of a kitchen drawer. There's a wall switch for the ceiling light. There are two lamps on the desk. She's not worried about a California brownout, a New York City blackout, a Theban world lit only by fire. She's not cowering in a basement waiting for bombs to fall. She's just burning at both ends.

The candle sits draped in dust on the edge of a shelf, an intricate story etched into its cylindrical body. There's a puff of clouds in one curved corner moving away from the town square. At the far end, just beyond the café's sidewalk tables and the cobbled road that wanders off between half-timbered building facades, the steepled church lords over the flowering planters in every window. Ornate lampposts define the unlit and the undark of a town etched into wax.

She enters the church's heavy iron-banded oak doors criss-crossed and studded with heavy nails. She faces a transcendent hallucination or lavish nightmare, the gilded leaf and scroll work built so high it would take a month of raking or a bomb to clear it out. In the souvenir shop on the corner, she buys a shot glass with this same view of town and café, but the church is missing. What surprises her is the small cemetery huddled between the church wall and the courtyard, as if they didn't believe this living and dying could go on for so long. Votive candles blacken a side room ceiling.

On the other side of Thebes, Stella drives by a
museum of sorts that has one reclining wax figure.
She stops and finds it doubles as a grocery store. The
walls are covered with yellowed newspaper clippings
claiming and reclaiming fading fame. She tries to read
as the brittle words fall off the pages. In the back
room, past the catcher's mitt-sized cans of outdated
tuna, five gallon tins of cooking oil, boxes of saltines
stacked shrine-like to the ceiling, cordoned by a
theater's velvet rope that guides the weeping and the
thrilled to a large brass plaque and beside it an open
casket. An idle air conditioner sits in the wall. The
face not decomposed but half-melted, oozes over the
white collar and onto the suit. From the sculpted,
swept-back, jet black hair, a smeared face stares up
from a wickless wax pool, lips parted to sing
Heartbreak Hotel.

Burning Bed

In a very old book, Sinbad is carried off by a hulking
bird of prey, its claws sunk into his shoulders, his legs
in motion. When hunger arrived he learned not just to
kick for his life but to run on air.

Prometheus delivered to the rock above all other
rocks of pain. The vultures clacked their beaks in a
slow dirge, each day circling and returning to
excavate his body. Prometheus alive to his own feast.

Sinbad escapes and sails into epic petty adventures.
Prometheus never rises from his extravagant
nightmare. He gave away too much: a taste for
charred flesh, a small warmth, a smaller circle of
safety.

Beyond the bed lamp's glow the sphinx's eyes glitter.
Stella warms her hands on mythic men then turns
back to Jake's dull flame.

RSVP

The invitation: embossed sun radiating slivers of gold
out to the edge of the card, the world flat, and Stella
half believes she's falling off, but chance is stupid,
luck dumb, coincidence always tripping into accident,
and she waited too long to respond.

The envelope sits on the table licked closed by
humidity, absent of a neatly folded optimistic note
and apology besides, containing less than a thimble of
air.

According to a statistics book left on her desk, for no
valid or reliable reason, there's an atom of oxygen
caught in this envelope that Sophocles once exhaled.

Laureate or not, there's not enough entombed for one
breath, certainly not for bride, groom, and guest.
Stella can't go and that leads her away from Daytona
Beach on the Gulf of Corinth, that place where the
soon wedded will fly featherless into the sea after the
partiers and blind seers have passed out.

Unemployed in Troy

Frustrated. All Jake's got is a rickety sawhorse that's stood for years in the yard. A Trojan horse of rot surrendering to the first Greeks that appear. He's adrift in a Sargasso of junk.

Unresolved. Jake leans on the humid air, ready to collapse into anyone's salty hands. Forget the doves and olive branches, just trickle-down arm-pit here. He declares the ark of the new world and no one signs up for a tour of duty.

Cantankerous. The wind keeps blowing promises. Shirt a sweaty spinnaker, flesh cutting a flaccid wake. Moorless. Shipless. The storm beats mosquito-infested puddles senseless.

Katzenjammered. Going nowhere fast, Jake wrestles the air. He bullies the flies on his infested stretch of beach. He drags the sawhorse into the house. He throws a stained sheet over it. The sail gallops in the box fan's exertions. Another summer shipwrecked swatting flies, waiting for a ship to return the wounded to Thebes.

Odyssey

A bare bulb hangs from the center of the ceiling like the condemned at a public execution. The Inquisition begins with the flip of a wall switch. In his second-hand stuffed chair, haunted by years of abandoned gods, Jake's enthroned, planting the flag, declaring new kingdoms for the realm as he channel surfs the shores of Lexus, Tide, Aleve, Coors, fabled lands far away from the Straits of Euripos and global warming.

Jake drifts between the peeling walls of another night. Sleep unreachable. There's still a life to discover, not to save. It's a gathering madness, channel to channel, pacing the blurred bridges of unwakefulness, weathering the electronic waves, wheel and rudder of the remote clutched in his sea-wracked hands, listening to wind whistle through the ragged rigging of the window screens.

It could be the fine remnants of stars banging against the window. It could be the code of a mystery cult revealing its secrets. It could be fat, dumb, june bugs manic in their insistence, persistent beyond survival. They hurdle against the glass to reach their 60 watt god, the sill littered with their sacrifices.

Double-Yoked

Rain dissolves the bedroom windows. Glass puddles
and glistens over the deck. Sirens and a storm arrive.
Every house in south county stricken. Dawn smeared
across the horizon, through the trees. Stripped of
leaves, branches hold nothing of the coming year
back. Wind-shredded, thunder-struck, lightning-
gouged, sleep alludes desire. In Magna Graecia,
before the Krotons invaded, the city of Sybaris
outlawed roosters within its walls. The citizenry slept
late through maelstroms.

Today the alarms are driven by prophecy and the
hour's plucked gears. The face in the window
balloons, set upon by a frenzy of hair. The face streaks
into a hundred chased droplets. Eyes blind ponds.
Jake turns away, resurrects himself in the kitchen. The
iron skillet an over-heated underworld. The first
cracked egg spills two yokes. A reptile book left open
on the table pictures a two-headed bull snake. We are
always on the lookout for monsters.

Agog

It's from the doctor who can't write another diagnosis on his knees.

It's from the draft board declaring the war daily and everywhere.

It's evangelical, telling him to dress in an envelope addressed directly to Olympus.

It's a forty-day-and-night cloud drowning his loud desires.

Stella Confesses to the Invention of Thebes

I heard the fans' spin and hum from the apartment
above, the machinery of air mocking me, never
wearing out as one bladed revolution followed
another, and it was not my own.

Through time's blur, I walk along the Agora past the
Blue Note, its doors closed and the rock n' roll inside
striking an extravagant repose till dark. I'm one step
ahead of the rumor that is always about to catch up
and tap me on the shoulder. This time it jumps ahead,
crossing rivers, mountains, cities, new-plowed fields,
to announce my arrival, but it's been years since I was
last in this town, though the way friends talk my
shadow is still wet on the sidewalks.

Only I understood that this town, and all the others,
invented me as they were my inventions: the bars
broken over the backs of blind nights, listening to the
clink of ice in the bottom of glasses flushing out
another morning, the high facades of Midwestern
main streets that led nowhere but the middle west of
Thebes, the alleys where I leaned against walls,
willing them to stand as those dirt-red bricks willed
my standing for another minute, and at last the
manicured parks after the ball field lights were turned
off, where I lie down into others' green histories.

All written there at my desk, where the tip of a
peacock feather, sprouting from a vase, caught a

slight breeze, the wake of my arm, as I reached to turn a page. I wasn't startled as the iridescent blues and greens called forth a jungle clearing, a gleaming machete, as the feather fluttered off the desk, and when I leaned forward to search the floor for its perch, it was gone.

In a town of inventions, so are a wife, a husband, a daughter and son, inventions, but the rumors didn't end; one day I nibbled lunch, as if I might turn ascetic, giving up all but an empty bowl and a few shreds of clothing to go begging for a world, but the young boy across the table, puzzled by the waiter's English, said, "There are Chinese people and there are Theban people," and following a thoughtful pause, "The rest are French." I knew that, as any child does before being excused from the table to run outside and press the dull blades of grass against his skin.

The day I walked up to the woman in the grocery, introducing myself out of the blue, that I was "Blue," and said I had dreamed her pushing a child in an otherwise empty shopping cart, her empty purse hanging from her shoulder, the basket's chipped chrome radiant, their faces glowing. I knew someday I would invent a child, memory tinkering and invention. I knew it was invention that left room for the living, if that is what it could be called as I added my name at the bottom of her crumpled shopping list.

In the book I once signed, a letter has disappeared from my name, leaving the rest of the signature fading, though the funny little picture I drew of a square two-story house on the single parabolic-pen-stroke of a hill, above the two squiggly lines of a river, cling to the page like the house clings to the smoke rising out of its chimney, which is blowing nowhere as it spreads over my name.

Today, over the paper plates heaped with potato salad and roast beef, ice cubes melting in Styrofoam cups, the sports banquet is steeped in self-congratulations: the best year, the best record, the best players, all that I would politely applaud, but even here over the waves of clapping and standing ovations, is a whisper of my flight into rumor, the tongue a poor perch for even one peacock feather.

One summer that will always be mine, all I could hear was the deafening scaffolds of crickets building around the house and the buffoon bullfrogs belching out the night. All I could see from the porch was one or two stars between the heavy canopy of leaves. A humid breeze blew through the branches, almost the pall of dark green chimney smoke, and that was enough, all I ever needed to drift away.

To see the sky smoked by the Milky Way, was to see the lewd, pale-glittering scar of hope, a feather that I swore each of us grasped, however loosely, that left me fluttering over ditches by back roads, where the wrong-turn, the deadend, was what I expected. To be greeted by the ebony howls of dogs beside patched together houses was just another step toward the room that is always found wanting, my imperfections necessary and sufficient for the life of invention, and this invention of leaving.

Another Theban Day

The Black Death has set sail for exurbia.
Anthrax just another valentine blurb.
Fed-ex is delivering smallpox to the front door.
Prairie dogs are burrowing through the floor.

The following poems are dedicated to:

New Waves on Old Water is dedicated to Steve and Reggie Tackett-Nelson

Amputee is dedicated to Stephen Wall-Smith

Middle Way is for Rick Goodman

Trouble With the Egyptian Travel Agent is dedicated to David Kelly

Stella Confesses to the Invention of Thebes is dedicated to Larry Levis.

Walter Bargen has published ten books of poetry, including *Harmonic Balance* (2001), *The Body of Water* (2003), and *The Feast* (2004). His poems and fictions have appeared in over one hundred magazines, including *American Literary Review, American Letters & Commentary, Beloit Poetry Journal, Denver Quarterly, Georgia Review, Missouri Review, New Letters, New Novel Review, Pleiades, Poetry East, River Styx, Seneca Review, Sycamore Review,* and *Witness*. He is the recipient of a National Endowment for the Arts poetry fellowship (1991); winner of the Hanks Prize (1995), Quarter After Eight Prose Prize (1996), the Chester H. Jones Foundation poetry prize (1997), and the William Rockhill Nelson Award (2005). He was appointed to be the first Poet Laureate of the state of Missouri (2008-2009).

CPSIA information can be obtained at www.ICGtesting.com
Printed in the USA
LVOW13s0346300114

371607LV00002B/31/P